Authorpreneurship 101

Write, Publish, & Sell Your Book Like a Pro

How-to Guide for Aspiring & New Authors

Written by Jessica LeeAnn

Authorpreneurship 101
Copyright © Jessica LeeAnn, 2019
Cover image: © Danny Media

Published by Chocolate Readings via KDP Publishing
www.chocolatereadings.com

ISBN-13: 9781794022140

Publisher's Note

I dedicate this book to every aspiring and new author who have the desire to have an amazing literary career and don't know where to start.

Table of Contents

Introduction

So, if you're reading this book you fall into one of the following categories: you aspire to write and publish a book, or you've written a book and aspire to turn your book into a business. Either way, know that you're reading the right book!

As you very well know by now, my name is Jessica and while I have a lot of titles that follow my name, the title I'm most passionate about is author. I absolutely *love* writing books! I wrote my first book in 2007 and published it in 2008. I did the whole try-to-find-an-agent thing, and submitted query letters to publishing companies - blah, blah, blah. After receiving *hella* rejection letters, I decided to try a different route.

I remember talking to one of my older cousins and telling her how frustrated I was about not getting my book published, and she told me about someone she knew who self-published their book. My eyes lit up and I couldn't *wait* to leave her house so I could see what this self-publishing thing was all about.

I remember going to my mom's house and researching a print-on-demand company called Lulu. That was the first day of the rest of my author life, because once I learned how to get my own book out into the marketplace it was on and poppin'!

Fast forward ten years and here I am not only publishing my 10th book, but I've since then have launched my own self-publishing and coaching business. I've been blessed to have helped dozens of other authors achieve their literary dreams, too. Dope, right?

Well, before I was able to teach others how to publish their own book, I ran into a lot of bumps, made numerous errors, and experienced many mishaps while learning about the industry on my own. Instead of being discouraged, I wrote down and continued doing the things that worked, and stopped doing what didn't.

I've made and recorded ten years' worth of mistakes in journals and various sticky notes that I keep in a tote. In 2017 I decided that I'll package what I've learned and teach other aspiring and new authors the right way to successfully write, publish, and sell books. I mean, I've finally figured it out, so why not?

Plus, I wish I knew someone who would have taught me how to start my author career for the price of a book. As a single mom, I wasn't always able to hire a coach. I know that this is the case for many other aspiring and new authors, too.

So! *Authorpreneurship 101* is for you. Yes, the you who have a dream to write a book, but don't know where to start. The you who want to publish your own book, but not sure which route to take. The you who published a book, but lack the sales and want to become the next Lisa Nichols or Derrick Jaxn and use your book to build a profitable business. Don't worry, with *Authorpreneurship 101* I got you!

So, what exactly is *Authorpreneurship 101*? It's an interactive guide to teach you how to write powerful content, choose the best publishing platform for your pockets, and how to build an author platform that will help you turn your book into a profitable business.

Are you ready to go from an aspiring or new author to a well-known, established, successful, money-making authorpreneur?

Grab a journal, a pen, and a highlighter. Take notes, study this guide, and implement the strategies that I'm sharing with you. I can guarantee, if you consistently follow and implement the techniques listed throughout this book and use the resources listed, you'll see the success you're looking for as an author.

Wishing you the best and sending positive literary vibes your way!

Jessica LeeAnn

1

Conquer Your Content

So! You want to write a book. That's amazing! I celebrate you in advance. I know firsthand how great of an accomplishment it is to write a book. I also know firsthand how scary it can be to share your thoughts and creativity with the world. I'm so proud of you for being bold enough to share your imagination or story with complete strangers. They won't be strangers for long, though. They'll be your favorite literary homies.

Okay, so there are many steps to writing a good book. A lot of writers know this, and sometimes feel a lot of pressure to write the perfect book, therefore they never get started. While it is important to write great content, don't put too much pressure on yourself. Doing so will cause you to overthink and then you'll lose the writing battle.

It's possible to write great content, but it's a process. The first thing you want to do is conquer your content. What does this mean? It means that you need to master your writing skills so that you can create content that will be enjoyable to your readers.

One of the ways you can conquer your content is by writing every day. Yep, you read that correctly. Write *every* day. You don't have to do this for hours on end. You can start with fifteen minutes a day and increase your time. Just be sure to stick with your minimum time frame to train yourself to write for a designated period.

Now, there are two ways that you can master your skills by writing every day: journaling or blogging. I *love* journaling. Journaling is simply writing your thoughts in a notebook. This method is quick and easy; and can be done anytime throughout the day that you can have at least fifteen minutes to yourself. Blogging is the cousin of journaling. Instead of writing in a notebook, you'll type up your thoughts. Both are great options. Choose the format that you're comfortable with and stick to it. Now, blogging will take up more of your time, but it's still a great way to strengthen your writing skills. Blogging is one of the ways that a lot of authors learn how to engage with their readers. It's easy to start, and there are plenty of free blog websites that you can take advantage of. You can check these options out:

➢ Blogger

- Wordpress
- Tumblr

Now, if you choose to blog, don't feel pressured to make your blog public. You can keep it private. This is simply a way to enhance your writing. However, if you're planning to build a platform, when you're comfortable, you can start sharing your blogs to gain readership. We'll talk more about that in a different chapter.

The main takeaway is this: journaling or blogging will teach you how to discipline yourself, expand your vocabulary, and how to focus on one specific topic or subject.

Once you conquer your content by way of journaling or blogging, the book writing process will go a lot smoother for you. You will also feel much more confident about what you produce, thus making your readers enjoy your amazing book.

Why Do You Want to Write A Book?

Books are by far one of the best ways to express yourself, share information, enlighten your tribe, as well as learn a new skill. Books are also a great way to entertain yourself. They're tools to impact and influence the masses. A book can be a small blueprint of how to implement what you know, or an intriguing collection of pages that tells a riveting story. The point of writing a book is to clearly share a story, message, lesson, or skill.

There are millions of people who desire to write a book. And I have to ask: why?

Are you writing a book because you have something powerful to say? Maybe you have a vivid imagination and want to share it with the world. What's your why? Knowing this will help you develop content that your readers will enjoy.

In order to impact, entertain, or influence your readers, you must know what you're going to say to them and why you're saying it. Readers do not like being confused by your content. They want, and expect, the content to be clear, concise, impactful, and practical.

So, before you start writing your book, whether fiction or nonfiction, you'll want to clearly define the core message (or story line) of your book. You need to have something to say that will enlighten, empower, entertain, or edify your readers.

Now that you know this, ask yourself: why do I *really* want to write a book?

What's Your Genre?

As you're figuring out why you're writing a book, this is the perfect time to define what *kind* of book you're going to write. In the literary world, writing about a specific topic or category is referred to as your genre.

Not sure what genre you write? No problem. A good way for you to know is to make a list of adjectives that represents the message of your book. What are some key emotions that are tied to your writing? How do you want readers to feel? Knowing these questions can help you understand your genre. You can also research other books that are similar to yours.

Your book may even cross genres, and that's fine. Here is a list of the most popular types of book genres:

- Fiction
- Nonfiction
- Novels
- Science fiction (Sci-Fi)
- Romance
- Mystery
- Fantasy
- Young adult
- Erotica
- Thriller
- Children's literature
- Urban fiction
- Historical
- Horror
- Crime
- Memoir
- Suspense
- Autobiography
- Self-help

If you're still unsure of the genre you write, stick with one of the basics, which is fiction or nonfiction. However, you'll want to chose a genre, because people will ask you and you don't want to stumble when asked.

Define Your Core Message

Before you start writing your book, focus on clearly stating what your book will be about. You want to have a core message so that when you start promoting your book, you will know who your target reader is and your target readers know that your book is for them.

Not sure what your core message is? Think about what you want your readers to walk away with after completing your book. What are you known for? Most knowledgeable about? What do you enjoy talking about? Keep these things in mind when thinking of what to convey to your ideal reader.

Here is an example of clearly defining your core message:

Authorpreneurship 101 is a how-to guide for aspiring and new authors which teaches practical and affordable ways to write, publish, and sell a well-written and polished book.

As you can see in the example used, I let the readers know that *Authorpreneurship 101* is a guide that will teach them something about how to write a book. So, clearly this book will be for people who are interested in writing and selling books.

Defining your core message will make it easy for potential readers to decide if your book is something they're interested in or not.

After you define your core message, you can now move on to creating an outline that aligns with the message of your book. which we'll cover in depth in a different section.

Educate or Entertain

As you've seen in the previous pages, there are so many genres to write about. Once you decide on your genre, decide if you'll write a book that educates or entertains. Sure, you can do both, but a book that is clear and concise will have a strong focal point on one area. It doesn't matter which genre or topic you chose, just make sure that the content you create will either transform and positively impact their thinking, or entertain them tremendously.

Once you decide why you're writing, decide what you want your readers to feel after reading your book. Do you want them to feel enlightened? Do you want them to feel entertained? Depending on your response, here are two checklists to ensure that you're creating content that will make a great impression on your readers:

> **To Enlighten**:
>> o Include exercises, techniques, and resources that aligns with the message of your book.
>> o Ask questions to make your readers think.
>> o Share the strategies you used to enlighten yourself.
> **To Entertain**:

o Include jokes and anecdotes; make them laugh or feel sensual.
o Be descriptive; make your reader feel as if they're in the scene with your characters.
o Be sincere by writing vulnerable, gut-wrenching words. Make your reader feel connected.

After someone reads your book, they should feel like their minds have been transformed, either from an educational or entertaining stand point. When you use these tips, your readers will remember how your words impacted or amused them.

I remember reading *Friends and Lovers* by Eric Jerome Dickey back in the early 2000's and that's still the most memorable book I've ever read. It entertained me tremendously. I laughed, cried, felt sensual, and connected to his characters and storyline. He is the reason why I wrote my first short story. Give your readers this same energy.

To Hire A Ghostwriter Or Not....

It's no secret that all authors aren't necessarily the strongest writers. This is why editors and ghostwriters are prominent in the literary industry. Now, don't be offended if you're not a strong writer. You can still be a successful author.

Let's be clear: there is a *huge* difference in someone being a writer and being an author. There are some that are both, but most of your favorite authors have hired a ghostwriter or has a really, really dope editor.

Nothing wrong with this.

Some people are better storytellers, thus they hire a ghostwriter to transcribe their story and turn it into a manuscript that is later published as a book. There are some people who are exceptional writers, but not great at conveying their message in a way that compels and captures the attention of a large audience.

If you're a great storyteller and not that strong of a writer, then it's better to hire a ghostwriter to help you craft your content and publish a powerful or insightful book, rather than to have an ego and try to write a mediocre book on your own.

Most authors get into this business because they have an impactful or transformational story or skill set to share, and plan to build an empire using their book (smart move by the way). If you're someone who falls into this category, don't be ashamed to hire either a ghostwriter or an amazing editor who can translate your content in a way that will bring you the success you desire as an author.

As we move forward to the next phase of the writing process, take some time to think about the content you just read. The most important thing I want you to remember is to conquer your content. Make sure you put in the effort to master your writing skills so that when you're ready to start working on your manuscript, your confidence exudes from the pages and pierce the hearts of your readers.

Up next: let's create your writing outline

2

Create a Writing Outline

I've had quite a few consultations with aspiring authors who've never published the book that's sitting on their mental shelf because they don't know where to start. They have no clue on how to develop a concept, writing outline, or chapter topics. This chapter will cover just how to do that.

So here's the deal: you can have a great idea or powerful testimony that can become a powerful book, but without fully developing the concept for your book, you will have a difficult time completing your story.

Over the next several pages, I will explain the process that you should follow to help you complete your first draft in 90 days. *90 days?* Yes, 90 days!

So, you have an idea (or three) about an amazing book. You have perfect techniques to share, some amazing strategies that work, an entertaining storyline, or a powerful testimony that will change or impact the lives of thousands of people.

You have a great, catchy title, some awesome quotes, a unique writing style, strong narratives, and transformational content that is going to change the game.

You've worked up the courage to share the content that you have. You've even set the time aside to get your writing done. You are ready! The problem is: this is all within your mind because you don't know where to start.

So many future authors get stuck with how to get started and become flustered with the entire process. Instead of giving up, what you want to do is create a writing outline. This will help you compartmentalize your thoughts and get clear on what you want to write about, as well as get a deeper understanding of what your book is really about. Let's delve into what it takes to create a good writing outline.

The first step to writing a good outline is to know exactly what your book is about. I recommend that all outlines start with the core message because it will help you develop chapter topics that relate to the topic of the book. Think of your core message as the main point (we covered this in the previous chapter).

Your chapters will be the major points that relate back to your book's core message aka the main point. The sub-topics will be minor points that relate back to the chapter, which is one of the major points of the book.

Still with me? Okay!

Your outline will remind you that the core message is the main point that you want to relay to your readers. Sure, you'll talk about different topics throughout your book. However, your chapter topic and sub-topics should always direct your readers back to your core message. These are all things that you will develop when writing your outline.

Before I learned how to create an outline, I was all over the place with my writing. Then one day I was told by a mentor to create an outline. Like *duh*, right? Well, I was in the dark once myself so I know how you feel about this process. Stay with me, I have you covered.

Creating an outline for my books has been such a blessing. One of the amazing things that I discovered about creating an outline is that I tend to finish my books more quickly. I mean, who wants to struggle with finishing their masterpiece? I sure don't! So outlines are my journalistic besties.

One of my favorite things about having a clear outline of what to write about is that it will help you when writer's block tries to rear its ugly head. You can always refer back to your outline to get you back on track so that you can complete your draft within the 90 day time frame you're striving for.

There are five key steps you'll need to take in order to complete your writing outline. Let's go over these steps:

➢ **Develop the message of your book.** So, you have an idea or concept for a book, but you really aren't sure how to turn your idea into a manuscript. What is the book about? How will you turn this into words that people can relate to? Answering these questions will help you develop your core message.

➢ **Create your chapter topics.** As mentioned before, your chapter topics should direct your readers back to your core message. The topics you want to talk about should be advice or wisdom that can help the reader better understand and relate to your core message.

   o When developing chapter topics, clearly state what subjects you are knowledgeable about or want to share with your readers. Don't focus on the length, just the value you want to bring.

You can change titles later when you're going through the editing process. I recommend creating at least eight.

➢ **Create sub-topics.** Sub-topics are minor points that supports that main or chapter topic. Again, these points or sub-topics should re-direct the reader back to the core message of your book. The sub-topics should align with the main topic or expand on your message for that specific chapter or topic.

   o Subtopics are powerful for nonfiction books because they allow you to diversify your brand.

Check out the example below of how a chapter & sub-chapter outline should look:

Chapter Topic 1: *How to write a book in 90 days.*

Sub-chapter topics

- *Create an outline*
- *Select a word count limit*
- *Set a tentative completion date*
- *Schedule 4-5 writing days each week*

➢ **Write your synopsis.** Now that you know what your book will be about, let's create the synopsis. What exactly is a synopsis? A synopsis is a detailed outline of your book. The easiest way to create a full synopsis is to write a short summary of each chapter. The summary should be 1-2 sentences long max. Merge the chapter summaries and BOOM! You have a synopsis. Your synopsis should be between 1,500 - 2,000 words. Be brief, yet captivating. *Tip: check out synopses of books that are in the same genre as your book for an idea.*

➢ **Write your book summary**. Most authors confuse their book summary with their synopsis. That's because they're siblings. A book summary is basically the little sister of the synopsis. It's the message that you put on the back of your book to explain what readers can expect when they purchase your book. Your summary shouldn't be more than three short paragraphs.

➢ **Choose a daily word count.** Okay, so another important phase of creating and using an outline is having a daily word count. As adults, we're all busy, and finding time to sit and write a book isn't as easy as one thinks. The best thing I discovered was setting a daily word count. If daily is too much for you, start with a weekly word count and progress.

See the following page for an example of how your writing outline should look and a word count chart.

Writing Outline

Core message: What readers can expect upon reading your book.

Chapter Topic: Main points that readers should connect back to core message of your book.

Sub-Topics: Content that supports your main point.

Summary: Brief description about your book; normally reserved for the back of your book.

Synopsis: Lengthy and detailed summary of your book.

Set a word count:

Overall	Weekly	Daily
25,000	2,100	300
30,000	2,500	360
35,000	3,000	430
40,000	3,340	480
45,000	3,750	535
50,000	4,170	595
55,000	4,585	655
60,000	5,000	715

If you're a fiction writer, your outline will be a little different. Your outline will include character development, having a protagonist and an antagonist, a scenery, etc. The next few pages will talk about how an outline for a fiction book should include.

Define Your Concept. So, the concept of your book is your idea. This could also be known as your storyline. Think of this as the reason why you are writing on this specific topic. What story do you want to share with the world?

You can develop your storyline by answering the following questions:

> ➢ Who is the main character or protagonist?
> ➢ What's his/her situation?
> ➢ What problem will be solved by the end of the book?
> ➢ Who will help the protagonist solve their issue?
> ➢ Who is the antagonist?
> ➢ What role does the antagonist play in the life of the protagonist?
> ➢ How will the issue be solved?

Decide on the Main Scenery. Now that you know who the story is about and what will take place, *where* will the story mainly take place? Make sure that you choose a place that compliments that main character's personality and issue. Research the location so that you can use realistic scenarios when developing your story. If your main character's form of therapy is to go to the beach, they can't live in a state that doesn't have easy access to the beach.

Develop Your Characters. This is the most important part of your book. Your characters must be realistic, relatable, and entertaining. Here are a few key points to keep in mind when developing your characters:

> ➢ Create a catchy name
> ➢ Describe how the character looks
> ➢ What is the age of the character?
> ➢ Where does the character work?
> ➢ Where does the character live?
> ➢ What type of car does the character drive?
> ➢ How does the character dress?

Be Creative. Since you are writing fiction, you can be as creative as you want. Go there! Be quirky, be unique, and be different. Try not to be predictable. Your content should be entertaining and engaging. Your goal is to write page-turning words that make your readers ask you for the next book. Here are a few ways that you can be creative:

> ➢ Think of a storyline that hasn't been done
> ➢ Insert surprise elements
> ➢ Develop characters that are flawed

Whether you're writing fiction or nonfiction, you want to be sure to write an outline. Having an outline will hold you accountable, as well as help you stay on track with your content. I can't tell you how many times I've had to go back to one of my outlines to remind myself of the direction I want my story to go!

So, now that you know how to create an outline and why you need it, are you ready to create your writing outline?

Up next: let's get prepared to publish

3

Prepare for Publishing

I know how exciting it can be to finally get that book out of your head, into a word document, and finally into a completed manuscript to be published. You can see yourself holding the book, signing the book, selling the book. And it's an *amazing* feeling.

Before you publish your book, there are a few key things to research and steps you'll want to complete. There are several things you need to check out, but there are three major parts of the publishing process that you do *not* want to skip over.

These three elements will save you time, stress, frustration, and your coins. Without the proper research and knowledge, you can waste a lot time that you can't get back. And you know how frustrating it can be to waste time and money. So to avoid that, check out three significant things that you want to do before taking the big step:

➢ *Invest in a professional editor*

➤ *Calculate the fees associated with publishing*
➤ *Hire a professional book cover designer*

Now, these three things may seem small, but trust me they're not. Having a badly edited book, not having a publishing budget, or having an unpleasing book cover can ruin your author reputation. Don't forget, first impressions are everything! You do not want people to read your book and see misspelled words, horrible formatting, or a bad storyline.

Do yourself a favor and don't skip over these procedures. You'll thank me later. Or now (smile with me).

Finding the Right Editor

A lot of first time authors skip over the editing process because 1) they can't find anyone and 2) because of the fees. I want to encourage you with a lot of tough love: no matter how much it costs you, hire a professional editor.

If you're going the self-publishing route, you need to factor in a budget for your editing. It's free to upload your own manuscript, so use the money you would have used to pay a hybrid or vanity publisher and hire a really great editor.

You might struggle with knowing where to find an editor, and if they'll be worth your money. Let me answer that question for you: it's worth the money.

You'll want to interview several editors to make sure they're a good fit for your book project. When you hire the right editor, you won't feel so bad about the fee.

Okay, so here are a few questions to ask a potential editor:

> *Are you comfortable with my genre?*
> *What's your turn around time?*
> *How many revisions will there be?*
> *What's your method of communication?*
> *What type of editor are you?*
> *Do you charge per page, word count, by the hour, or a flat rate?*

With freelancing being a huge thing right now, it's pretty easy to find an affordable, and professional editor. You can check out websites such as:

> Fiverr
> Upwork
> Elance

I encourage you to read reviews, and also ask other authors who edited their books.

You Charge How Much?

So, let's address this mountain: editing is going to cost you a pretty penny. Editing is not a cheap service. Like, at all. So many first-time authors cringe when they hear the fees and often try to edit their own books. Please don't be this author. Close your eyes and pay the fee.

As an editor myself, I am a little biased about the fees we charge. You're probably thinking, *but why so much?* Because it's a tedious and time consuming activity. Rewarding, yes. Entertaining, definitely; but very tedious.

So, how much can you expect to pay? Well, it depends on the editor. There are four ways that editors can charge: a flat rate, per hour, per word, or per page. Let's see what each of these pricing options look like.

Per Hour	$25 - $85
Per Word	$.08 - $.18
Per Page	$3 - $5
Flat Rate	$250 +

How do you know what to pay? After you find out what the editors you interview are charging according to your word or page count, you'll be able to make a more informed decision.

The Different Types of Editing

Okay, so there are four different types of editing that your manuscript will need: proofreading, formatting, copy, and developmental. You'll need to understand what type of editing is best for your project, so you can determine which editor will be the best fit.

Editing isn't just a one-time deal, either. It happens in phases. There will be quite a bit of back and forth when you're in this stage of your project. So I'm cautioning you in advance: be patient.

There are some editors who are well-versed in all four areas. However, most editors are only strong in 1-2 of these areas. It's your responsibility as the author to 1) understand what you need and 2) to find the right person. Don't be afraid to ask for samples of their work. Let's talk about the different types of editing.

Proofreading

This form of editing is not as intense, but just as important as the other three forms. Proofreading detects minor errors such as grammar and style, capitalization, punctuation, spelling errors, and word usage. This type of editing should be done prior to formatting.

Formatting

This form of editing is required to shape your manuscript into print-ready mode for publishing. It's also known as interior layout. This is the finishing touches on your manuscript which transitions into a book during printing. This should be the last stage of editing.

Copy editing

This form of editing includes correcting your grammar, style, duplication, word usage, and verbiage. This style of editing is also known as line-by-line. It's an intense review of your content. The purpose of this style of editing is to polish your content to produce a well-written manuscript. This is the most popular, and important type of editing.

Developmental editing

This form of editing is the most rigorous stage of revising your manuscript. It includes closely evaluating your entire manuscript and thoroughly reviewing the structure, organization, and consistency of your content. This process includes removing and/or adding sentences; paragraphs being rephrased, reduced, or extended. Sections of your content may be moved from one section to another to ensure the flow of your manuscript is cohesive. This is the most expensive type of editing. It's not crucial, but if you're a first-time author, I recommend this type of editing in conjunction with the others.

So! Now that you know what type of editing options are out there, this will help you decide which editor will be best for your project.

The Editing Process

Okay so, let's talk about what the editing process is truly like. It's not necessarily a fun process because you are basically turning in your passion project to be slaughtered and mended before being published. When you turn your manuscript over to your editor, here a few different things that will (or should) happen, and to keep in mind.

An editor will question the title and subtitles for your manuscript and chapters. Consider that when you're working with an editor, they are viewing your manuscript from a different perspective. I know that your content is near and dear to your heart, but the point of hiring an editor is so that they can dissect and polish the content that you wrote. Now, editing is not changing your story. This process is simply evaluating and elevating what you already submitted.

An editor will provide constructive criticism. The feedback may sting a little because you put your all into your first draft and here comes this person telling you that you need to change this or that. And yes, there will be many drafts until your final manuscript is completed. This person will honestly tell you about the flow of the book, as well as if the content aligns with the synopsis/theme of the book. Again, this does not mean the editor is responsible for changing your story. They are merely providing feedback. You will make the final decision to change your story or not.

Your editor is not perfect. Please don't put pressure on your editor while they are working on your manuscript. They're human ya know! Sure, you may find a few errors during the process, but be confident that your editor will turn in Grade A work when the process is final and complete. Remember, there will be several drafts before the manuscript is considered done. Also, most editors have proofreaders who will read your story to catch additional errors. I also encourage you to get a fresh pair of eyes to proofread on your end as well.

Be flexible with your editor. Turnaround times can fluctuate. Don't take this personal. This person more than likely has several projects that they're working on. This doesn't mean that they can't handle yours, there's just a hierarchy that needs to be followed.

Set a Budget

Okay, so when it comes to self-publishing, there are two options that you can choose. You can either hire someone to publish your book for you, or you can learn how to publish your book on your own. I'll go into more about this in the next chapter.

Whether you decide to publish your own book or hire someone to assist you, you will have to invest your coins. You'll need to pay for an editor of course, but you'll also need to pay for a book cover designer, and copies of your newly published book. You have the option of buying your own ISBN and bar code, or you can possibly get one for free with the print-on-demand company you sign up with. You'll also need to pay a fee to get your book officially copyrighted. Not to mention, you'll need to have a budget for promotion.

No matter if this is your first or tenth book, you'll need to financially invest into your marketing and promotional strategy at some point.

Okay, so now that you know for sure that you'll need to financially invest in your project, how much money are we exactly talking here? Now these fees are not set in stone. These are fees that I recommend that you don't exceed as a self-publishing author. So, let's break it down:

Editing fee	$250 - $1000
Book cover fee	$50 - $200
Self-publishing fee	Free*
ISBN + Bar Code fee	$55 - $125
Copyright fee	$85 - $140
Book Promotion fee	$40 - $200*

*Self-publish: Free (You'll need to incorporate the cost of printing your book and it also depends on the print-on-demand company you choose.)

*Book Promotion fees solely depend on the company and the frequency you use the services.

*Note these figures are estimates. These prices depend on the companies that assist you, as well as how elaborate the services are that you'll need.

So, you're looking at about $500-$1,000 to self-publish your own book. If you choose to hire someone, those fees start at about $1,000. Again, it depends on the company you choose and the quality of their services.

Designing Your Book Cover

When you are working with a book cover designer, please inquire about the type of covers they're capable of creating. This section will cover what questions you should ask your potential designer, as well as what you can expect.

If you're publishing a paperback or hard cover, you'll need a full cover with a spine, especially if your book is more than 100 pages. Your front cover should be the image you chose for your book that includes your book title and your author name. The spine should have your book title and your name, and the back cover should have a synopsis, short bio, your picture if you choose (I recommend this for branding purposes) and a space for your bar code and ISBN number.

The designer should be familiar with the different types of book cover templates. There are plenty of book sizes to use. However, 5 1/2 x 8 1/2 and 6 x 9 are standard book sizes to use in the publishing industry.

Expect to pay a minimum of $60 for a good, quality book cover. If you're getting an illustration, the minimum will be closer to $100. I know that you're self-publishing and your funds may be limited, but please don't skimp on the book cover design process. Despite what the saying is: your readers *will* judge your book by its cover, so pick a good one!

The designer you're working with should ask you the following questions before starting on your book:

- ➤ *What size is your book?*
- ➤ *How many pages is the book?*
- ➤ *Do you have your bio, picture, and synopsis?*
- ➤ *What is the color scheme for your book?*
- ➤ *What format is the book being published? (Paperback, e-book)*

If these questions do not arise during your consultation, move on to the next designer. Also, it will help if you mention to the designer what platform your book is being published through so they can design it accordingly.

If you're not sure what type of cover you should have, I recommend checking out other books in your genre to see what's selling. Unfortunately people are more inclined to buy a book that has a great cover, rather than an impactful title. So the choice you make can and will affect your book sales.

To Copyright or Not to Copyright?

I get this question a lot during consultations from aspiring authors: should I copyright my book? This section is going to answer this question, once and for all.

While your book is copyrighted the moment you write it, it doesn't protect you from copyright infringement. Copyright only stops another author from copying your content. Unfortunately it doesn't stop someone from creating the same concept or idea as you around the same time.

Okay, here's a not-so-fun fact: if two writer's come up with the same concept, at the same time, and both writers have no clue that the other is working on the same concept, then both would have equal claim to the copyright. Interesting, right?

In order to have complete ownership of your concept or idea, you'll need to register your book through the copyright office. Doing this will guarantee your ownership to your content. And then you won't have to fight anyone over your intellectual property.

Registering a copyright is pretty easy and straightforward. In order to register your book, you'll just need to go to copyright.gov and fill out the form. After you pay the fee, BOOM! You're manuscript is registered.

So, to answer the question at the beginning of this section: as an author, do you need to copyright your content? Yes, yes you do.

What Can You Copyright?

So! Now that you know that copyrighting is important, let's talk a little about what exactly you can or cannot copyright. In short, here are the things you *cannot* copyright:

➤ Names
➤ Titles
➤ Short Phrases
➤ Expressions

This means that you cannot copyright a catchy slogan you came up with for your author brand, book title, etc. Now, you can't copyright these things, but you *can* trademark them.

Now that you know what you cannot copyright, here is a list of what literary content that you can copyright:

➤ Poetry
➤ Novels
➤ Movies
➤ Songs

Once you submit your manuscript via the online registration, it will take about three months to be processed. If you choose to drop it in the mail, it can take up to ten months. I think we can agree the electronic way is best, right?

The takeaways from this chapter is to make sure you have a budget, hire an editor, a book cover designer, and submit your manuscript to the copyright office to avoid infringement.

I know this is a lot of information, but don't get overwhelmed. It's better to be informed than unaware. Now, let's get that book published!

Up next: the publishing process

4

Publish Like a Pro

Okay, so! Now that you are prepared to publish your new book, let's move past any fears and doubts, and make it happen!

In this chapter, we're going to discuss the different types of publishing methods, the difference between paperback, hard cover, e-book, and audio books, as well as the pros and cons of each publishing platform. Oh, you thought it was just one way to make your publishing dreams come true? Nope!

So, how many different ways can you actually get your book published? There are four ways to accomplish your goal of becoming an author. Let's dive into each method, along with the pros and the cons.

Traditional Publishing

Traditional publishing is the goal that every aspiring author strives for, and should. This type of publishing will put you in the big leagues! Having a traditional publisher means that one of the major publishing houses in the literary industry purchases the right to publish and sell your manuscript.

Depending on the size and status of the company, you could be offered a lucrative contract. Once your contract is signed, traditional publishers sell your book via booksellers such as Barnes & Noble, and other popular outlets.

Anyone who seals the deal with a traditional publishing company is legit! Signing with a traditional publisher means that someone within the company believes the content you wrote is marketable to the masses and will impact your tribe in a major way. What an accomplishment!

Fun fact: most traditional publishers only take on certain genres, which can be a little challenging. You'll need to do some digging to see what genres certain companies are accepting at the present moment, or if they're even accepting new manuscripts at all.

Now, it's not easy to get a publishing deal with a traditional publishing company, but it's definitely possible. These days, there's a criteria you'll need to meet in order to even get a conversation started with someone who works with a traditional publishing company. These companies are all about making money. So, if they feel you won't make the big bucks, they'll look over you.

Because social media is such a huge entity, most authors without a strong social media presence, brand, or influence, will have a really hard time landing a traditional publishing contract. Not only that, but there's a protocol you'll need to follow to get in the doors of one of these companies.

First, you will need a literary agent. What's that? A literary agent is a liaison between an author and a traditional publishing house. This individual reviews manuscripts, helps authors build the foundation for their careers, and negotiate contracts on the author's behalf. A traditional publisher will not accept a manuscript from an aspiring author if they do not have a literary agent. Period.

So, what does it take to get a literary agent? You'll have to pitch yourself to an agency. That means you'll need to create a synopsis for your book, submit a query letter, and include the first three chapters of your book in an email to the agent you're interested in. If the agent is accepting queries, they'll be the person who will help you get a publishing contract.

Before you do this, be sure to thoroughly research the agent to be sure that they'll be interested in your genre, and they're trustworthy.

Now, most aspiring authors believe that signing with a major publishing company means that their journey of Authorpreneurship will be easier, but that's not necessarily the case. You'd still be responsible for marketing and promoting your own book, with your own money. Hence, why most authors receive an advance.

Okay, so let's talk about the pros and cons of having a contract with a traditional publishing house.

Pros & Cons of Traditional Publishing

As with anything, there are pros and cons to having a traditional publisher. Below you'll see the most common pros and cons:

Pros:

- You'll have major distribution
- There's a possibility you'll receive an advance

- It'll be a lot easier to get publicity

Cons:

- You'll lose the rights to your manuscript
- You'll have to split your royalties
- You will lack of creative control over your career

Vanity Publishing

Vanity Publishing is when you pay an independent company to publish your manuscript for you, or you pay to contribute to an anthology. You can also pay for additional services such as editing, book cover design, branding tools, marketing services, etc.

Unlike traditional publishers, vanity publishers usually will publish any type of book. While some people look at this from a negative perspective, I don't see this as a negative thing. There are a lot of aspiring authors who have great books. However, because of the nature of the traditional publishing industry, most of these authors will never see mainstream success. It's vanity publishing companies that make it possible for unknown authors to achieve their literary goals.

Here's a hard truth: the reason that most vanity publishing companies have a negative energy associated with it is because most companies take advantage of aspiring authors. These companies have been known to produce low-quality work, and overcharge authors to print copies of their book in bulk.

However, not all vanity publishers are out to get you. Some actually have quality products and affordable prices. I believe that there are more integrity-based vanity publishers who are helping to change the narrative. If you choose to go this route, thoroughly do your research.

I actually used a vanity publisher when I contributed my work to an anthology a few years ago. It was a very positive experience.

Pros & Cons of Vanity Publishing

Most people will not admit that there are any pros to vanity publish, but I disagree. See below for the pros and cons of choosing a vanity publisher.

Pros:

- You'll successfully publish your book or contribute your work to an anthology

- You have the option to choose an affordable plan
- You'll receive higher royalties

Cons:

- You'd be taking a risk of receiving low-quality work
- It's possible that you will have lack of exposure
- The printing costs could potentially be high

Hybrid Publishing

Hybrid publishing is similar to vanity publishing. While you will have a fee, this type of company usually is selective about the type of content they publish. Think of a hybrid publishing company as a mix of traditional and vanity. This option gives you the best of both worlds.

While you may have to cover the cost of publishing upfront with a hybrid publisher, majority of these types of publishing companies give you 100% of your royalties, unlike a traditional or vanity publisher. Sure, you'll be responsible for paying for your own editor and book cover designer. However, you will be in full control of how much money you charge for your book and the amount of royalties you get.

A hybrid publisher also provide its authors with professional and high-quality marketing services and branding tools. This type of company usually have literary connections that benefit their authors, which leads to a successful career.

Pros & Cons of Hybrid Publishing

I am partial to hybrid publishing because my company, Chocolate Readings, is a hybrid publishing company. However, I have to be fair and provide the pros and cons of choosing a hybrid publishing company for your literary career. See below:

Pros:

- You're more likely to produce a high-quality book
- You'll receive 100% of your royalties
- Your book will be professionally edited, and you'll have access to quality marketing services

Cons:

- You'll have to pay upfront for literary services
- There's a risk of not getting your full investment right away
- It could be challenging to reach your ideal readers

Self-Publishing

Self-publishing is the path that has allowed many, many people to accomplish their literary dreams, including me. Taking this path of publishing means that the author will need to solely rely on themselves from start to finish.

Although it is a lot of hard work, and an intricate process, I'm a huge advocate for this method of publishing. I recommend doing as much research about the process prior to jumping in feet first. While some parts of the self-publishing process is quite simple, it's best to learn the ins and outs before wasting time and money.

Now, some platforms, such as Kindle Direct Publishing or Lulu, allows self-publishing authors to upload and distribute their manuscript for free. However, you will need to purchase copies of your book once it's approved. Granted, you'll save quite a bit of money learning how to publish your own book, you'll want to be sure to financially invest in a professional editor, book cover designer, and book promotion plan.

It's important for you to understand that as a self-published author, you are in full control of your literary journey. This means you'll be responsible for finding your own editor, learning how to publish your own manuscript, marketing your own book, finding your own book cover designer, hiring your own publicist, etc.

Okay! So, let's go over the pros and cons of publishing your own book.

Pros & Cons of Self-Publishing

Pros:

- You'll have full creative control
- You'll receive 100% of your royalties
- You can publish books at your own pace

Cons:

- You'll need to invest in learning the process

- You'll need to invest in developing your brand
- Lack of experience could possibly produce low-quality work

ISBN + Barcode

Okay so, we've covered the types of publishing paths that you can take, let's get into the nitty gritty of the ins and outs of self-publishing. First up: ISBN and barcodes.

Every paperback or hard cover book that is being sold, or will be sold, needs a unique number known as an ISBN. The abbreviation for ISBN stands for International Standard Book Number. This unique thirteen digit code is located on the back of all printed books below the bar code.

So, what exactly is the ISBN number used for? It helps booksellers, libraries, and internet retailers identify your book so that it can be ordered, sold, listed, and sales can be recorded.

Now that you know what your ISBN is for, let's talk about the barcode. We've all seen this. It's on every product that's sold in the world. While they may all look alike, the barcodes found on books are different. They're referred to as a Bookland EAN.

The EAN is created based off of the ISBN that's assigned to your book.

When the bar code of your book is scanned, it picks up the detail about your book; that includes the title, genre, your name, etc.

Now, if your book is published in different formats such as paperback and hard cover, you'll need a different ISBN and barcode. Remember, the point of these items is to keep track of your sales, etc.

While your paperback and hard cover book will each need its own ISBN and barcode, an audio book and e-book does not require these items. However, if you want to keep track of your book sales outside of the print-on-demand company you launch your project with, I'd recommend getting an ISBN for these formats as well.

Types of Books

Now that we've talked a little about the logistics of self-publishing, let's talk about the next important level - the different book formats that you can actually publish. There are four different layouts that you can launch: an e-book, paperback, hard cover, or audio book. Let's break these categories down.

E-book. An e-book is an electronic version of a printed book that can be read on digital devices such as computers, tablets, and cell phones.

Paperback. A paperback book is when your printed manuscript is held together by a paperboard cover and glue. This type of book is the most popular of the categories.

Hard cover. A hardcover book is when your printed manuscript is held together with a higher quality of paper, a cover jacket, and usually are larger. The flexible spine that allows the book to lie flat when opened, is what differentiates it from a paperback book.

Audiobook. An audiobook is a recording of a manuscript that can be listened to through your computer, Bluetooth, or other digital device.

If you truly want to write a book, you have many options to choose from to get your book out into the marketplace. Don't let finances block you from pursuing your publishing goals. You can start with one format and then add the others as you move along your author journey.

Now that we've talked about the different types of publishing, the different book layouts you can publish, let's move on to how this is actually done.

What is Self-Publishing?

As you know, there are four ways that you can get your manuscript published. While all four ways are great, I am an advocate of self-publishing. Why? Because it is extremely hard for unknown, unpopular aspiring authors to get a publishing deal without the right platform or book agent.

I believe that there are a lot of stories that don't get told because they lack the platform. I am truly grateful for print-on-demand companies. Without them, I wouldn't have accomplished my own literary goals. So, having said that, I'll share with you the basics of how to get your book successfully self-published.

Self-publishing, also known as printing on demand, is a pretty simple process. However, it can be *very* tedious. You'll need to be patient and do a lot of research on the companies that offer self-publishing services.

There are two popular print-on-demand companies that caters to authors and indie publishing companies: Kindle Direct Publishing and Lulu. These two companies are user friendly and will be a great platform to learn the self-publishing process. Best of all: these platforms do not charge you to upload your manuscript, unlike their competitors. Let's talk a little more about these companies.

Kindle Direct Publishing

Commonly referenced in the literary industry as KDP, this platform allows authors to upload their manuscript and distribute their books through Amazon. Authors have the option to publish a paperback, e-book, or audiobook. Previously, Kindle Direct only published e-books and Createspace published paperback books. However, in 2018, Createspace was acquired by Kindle Direct Publishing. Most authors see this as a positive transition. To a degree, I second that. Rather than having two accounts, authors can publish all book formats under one account, which can be easier when it comes to tracking sales and receiving royalties.

Lulu

Lulu is very similar to Kindle Direct Publishing. It's also easy to publish your manuscript. However, Lulu offers a wider range of options for book formatting and distribution. Lulu's distribution includes Amazon, Barnesandnoble.com, Nook, Kobo, Apple iBookstore, and the Ingram network. Unlike KDP, Lulu gives you the option to print your book as a hardcover. You can also print journals, calendars, and photo books.

While these are my top two choices for first-time authors, here is a list of three other print-on-demand companies that you can use. The companies are very popular. However, they will require a fee to use their services:

> ➢ IngramSpark
> ➢ BookBaby
> ➢ Blurb

Now that you know about the different print-on-demand companies that are user-friendly and free for aspiring authors, I encourage you to dig a little deeper and choose the best option for you and your financial ability.

As far as the process, it's pretty much the same across the board. Each platform has a digital course that you can take to show you how to go through the publishing process. I encourage you to take these courses before you finish your manuscript so that you can know exactly what to expect, even if you decide to hire a Self-Publishing Consultant. Now, if you don't have the patience to learn the process or aren't as tech savvy, consider hiring a Self-Publishing

Consultant. If you choose this route, be prepared to invest a minimum of $1,000.

If you are patient enough to learn how to publish your own book, know that it will be difficult to make any major mistakes, so at least try it out. Print-on-demand platforms have restrictions, which makes it difficult to mess up. However, the issue isn't in the actual publishing process. Most authors make a mistake in what they do *before* publishing their book.

Self-Publish Checklist

Before you go through the publishing process, I want to reiterate hiring professionals to help you. You can perform the publishing process on your own. However, I want you to consider outsourcing for the other tasks. Make sure that you hire an editor, a proofreader, (sometimes this person can be one in the same); be sure to get your manuscript formatted in a layout that accommodates the margins for print-on-demand companies, as well as a graphic designer for your book cover.

Determine if you're going to purchase your own ISBN number or use the free one assigned by the print-on-demand company, if applicable. Remember, if you purchase your own ISBN number, you'll also need to purchase your own barcode.

Make sure that you have a cover designed to meet the specifications of the print-on-demand company that you choose. Lulu and KDP will be a little different, so make sure you mention this to the graphic designer that you consult with. Ask the designer if they are familiar with these types of layouts. If they're not, find another one.

If this is your first time self-publishing, it's possible that you'll make a mistake or two, or five, and that's okay. Don't beat yourself up about it, just adjust what you need to, and keep moving forward with the process. You got this!

Up next: let's develop your brand

5

Develop Your Brand

Something that I wish I knew before I published my first book in 2008 was the importance of having a brand. Since it took me a while to learn this lesson, this is the very first thing that I teach my clients. I encourage them to work on their brand *before* publishing their book. Why? Because for the most part, people only buy books from authors they know, trust, and like. I cannot stress this enough, literary homies. Develop. Your. Brand!

Once you get your author brand established, you can't just let it sit there. You have to work it! What does this mean? Staying consistent with sharing the message of your book, showing up as the expert on and off line, and positioning your platform in front of the right readers.

Having a brand as an author is just as important as your book. Without a brand, no one will feel connected to you. And if no one feels connected to you, you will not sell books. Harsh, but real.

Why do you need a brand? So you can sell books to more than your family, friends, and co-workers. Your author brand is what will proceed you, attract potential readers, and help you increase book sales.

Okay so, now that you know that you need a brand, let's define what exactly a brand is. It's how you express who you are as an author to the world. It's the things you say, post, and write about. It's the type of website you have, your social media engagement, the videos you share. It's the emotions that people feel when they see your books. It's *everything* about who you are as an author. And potential readers are watching you, darling!

Don't underestimate developing and establishing a unique brand. I'm telling you, your brand is what will get your book the exposure you desire.

Now that you know why you need a brand, let's talk about how to develop and get your brand established.

Seven Ways to Build Your Author Brand

As discussed in the previous section, before you can successfully sell books you'll need to focus on building your platform. Sure, you can sell a few books here and there to family and friends, but I'm sure that you didn't write a book just for family and friends. You have a message, whether fiction or nonfiction, that you want to share with the masses. In order to do that, people have to know who you are. People will only know who you are if you are visible in the marketplace, on and off line.

Below you'll find seven ways that can help you build your brand and position your platform in front of the right people.

1. **Identify Your Ideal Reader.** In order to build a strong brand and impactful platform, you have to understand who your book is for. While you may be an amazing writer, truth is, your book is *not* for everyone. Take the time to learn who your book is for.

2. **Develop Your Core Message.** What message do you want to relay to your readers? Whether you write fiction or nonfiction, you have something powerful that you want to communicate to your readers. When you're clear on your message, you can quickly find your ideal readers.

3. **Define Your Unique Selling Point.** What makes you stand out amongst your competition? There should be something unique about your brand that allows your ideal readers to find you in the midst of the crowd. Truth is, there are millions of other writers. It's your responsibility to develop a brand that captures the attention of your readers.

4. **Know Your Genre/Niche.** What type of content do you write? Fiction? Nonfiction? Memoirs? Self-help? You should be able to quickly tell someone the type of books you write. Knowing your genre or niche topic will help you market and promote your book to the right audience.

5. **Build Readership.** Establishing your platform takes time. This is done by strategically positioning yourself in front of your target audience and providing them with resources that are useful. Tools to build your readership includes: having a mailing list, freebies, sneak peeks of upcoming books, creating products or services that can support, assist, or teach your audience a new skill or technique.

6. **Invest in the Theme of Your Brand.** As an author, you'll need a website. Why? This is how readers will learn more about you as an author. Remember, people are not just buying your books, their buying who you are as a person. Your social media platforms, website, logo, and message all matters when building your brand.

7. **Be Consistent With Your Branding.** It's important to remain consistent with promoting and marketing your brand, book and platform. Make good use of social media, live streams, blogging, interviews, podcasts, online and live events. The only way for people to know who you are is to remain in their faces.

The one thing that I want you to remember when developing your brand is that your brand is the bridge that will connect your book to your target audience. And when your brand is positioned in front of the right people, you'll sell books.

Author Brand Checklist

Now that you have seven major ways to get your author brand started, let's go over the things you'll need to build your author brand.

Below you will find a checklist that will help you build your author brand. If you don't have these things, hop on it quickly. If you're still working on your brand, make sure you have all of these things mentioned below:

- Main logo (graphic or font based)
- Brand colors (choose two to three main colors)
- Brand fonts (one main or body font and one accent font)
- Brand tagline or signature phrase
- Website and/or Blog
- Social media accounts
- Facebook cover
- Professional headshot
- Business cards
- Signature graphics
- Book mock ups
- Domain name
- Professional email account

So! Now that you know a few key elements you need to get your author brand off of the ground, are you ready to make it happen?

I know it may seem unnecessary, but it's all a part of getting your brand established. Also, it's better to get these things out of the way before you step foot into the marketplace. Be aware that there are other authors out there already doing these things. You don't want to get looked over for not presenting yourself as a professional author.

Up next: let's find your ideal reader

6

Find Your Ideal Readers

I t doesn't matter how dope of a writer you are, or how powerful your content is; as briefly stated in the previous chapter: your book is not for everybody. Your job as an author is to find who your book is for before you craft a unique and captivating plan of action to draw them in. We're going to go in depth in this chapter in regards to finding the right readers.

Most new authors think that just because they have a message that will pierce the hearts of a certain group of people that they'll just come running to purchase your book after you click the publish button in Kindle Direct or Lulu. They won't. Not if they don't know who you are, or that you wrote a book for them.

Before you publish your book, you should have an ideal reader in mind. You should have an idea of the type of person who will be interested in what you have to say. This is critical when it comes time to market and promote your book.

So, how do you do that? Glad you asked! There are three ways that you can find your ideal readers.

Identify Your Ideal Reader

The first thing that you want to do is understand who will be reading your book. Ask yourself the following questions:

➢ *What problem am I solving for my reader?*
➢ *How will my content impact this reader?*
➢ *What makes my book stand out?*

Answering these questions will help you create marketing content that will draw your ideal reader to your platform. When you know who is reading your book, it will be much easier to draw them in with the message of your book.

Specific people are drawn to a specific energy. What vibes are you sending out when you talk about your book?

An important technique that you'll need to have to attract your ideal reader is reliability. You want to be sure that your readers feel connected to you before they purchase your book. Share your pain points. Talk about why you wrote the book. This will let them know that you've not only experienced what their dealing with, but you also have a solution that can be beneficial to them as well.

Connect with Your Ideal Reader

Once you understand who your book is for, now it's time to connect with them. In order to connect with your ideal reader, you're going to need a little bit more information about them. In order to find them, you'll need to create a Reader Avatar.

What in the world is *that*? It's a chart to help you understand who your ideal reader is and ways you can interact with them. This eliminates a lot of guess work when it comes time to promote your book. I want you to really understand that being a successful author is about thinking like an entrepreneur. If you want to sell your book, you need to know who is going to buy it first.

When you're creating your Reader Avatar, be *super* specific. I'll be honest: you'll need to get all in your potential readers' business. Why? Because you'll need to use their interests, personal habits, and pain points in your marketing message.

You'll need to craft a message that specific people will feel connected to. Your potential readers need to feel as if they can relate to you. Remember, you want your readers to feel like they know you, which will make them like you, and therefore trust the content that you write. This goes for any genre that you write.

The Reader Avatar will help you learn more about who'll be buying your book. Yes, it'll be a little invasive, but you'll need to go there so you can sell your books. Okay, ready to get in some people's business?

Check out the Reader Avatar on the following pages for an example.

Reader Avatar

Male or Female

Age group:

20-29
30-39
40-49
50-59
60+

Parental status:

No children
1-2
3-4
5+

Salary:

$25,000 - $35,000
$36,00 0 - $45,000
$46,000 - $55,000
$56,000 - $65, 000
$66,000 - $75, 000
$75,000 +

Book Preference:

Paperback
E-book
Hardcover
Audio book

Marital status:

Single
Married
Divorced

Social media preference(s):

Facebook
Twitter
Instagram
LinkedIn
Pinterest

Reader Avatar

Occupation

_____

_____

Geographical location

_____

_____

Interests

_____

_____

_____

_____

Pain points

_____

_____

_____

_____

Challenges

_____

_____

_____

_____

Okay! Now that you know how to identify your ideal reader, and you know how you can connect with them, let's talk about how you will position your book in front of them by way of engagement.

Engage With Your Ideal Reader

We both know that you didn't write a book just so that it can sit on the virtual or physical book shelves. You want to sell your book to people that will find value in your content. While this should definitely be an end goal, it shouldn't be your main focus.

I know this is going to sound crazy, but don't try to sell your book immediately to potential readers. I'm sure you're thinking, *did I just read that last sentence correctly?* Yep, you did.

Here's the thing, you want to build a reputation of being established in your writing niche before you ask someone to buy a book from you. This part of the literary journey is spilling over into branding, which we'll talk about in depth in the next chapter. But before we do, I want you to understand what being an authorpreneur is really about.

Now, if you just want to write books for profit, by all means, flat out ask people to buy your books. And let me know how that works out for you.

If you want to be a successful authorpreneur with long-term success, you're going to need to learn how to engage with your ideal readers. You'll also need to learn how to sustain a relationship with them so that when you write and publish more books, you'll have a guaranteed audience who will be ready to purchase your books.

So, how do you engage with your readers? Here are three easy, and fun ways to stay interactive with readers, potential and existing:

1. **Be active on social media**. Create posts that gets your audience excited. Ask questions, play games, have fun!
2. **Share excerpts of your writing**. Whether it's the current book you're promoting, an old one, or just a blog post.
3. **Ask for their opinion**. Let them in on future writing topics you're considering. Let them feel as if they're a part of your writing journey.

Your goal should be to show readers why your content is amazing. Keep in mind that you want to be likable and relatable. Also, your persona should embody the content that you write. If you write inspirational or spiritual content, show that. If you write funny fiction novels, share jokes. If you write erotica, be sensual. Don't just talk about what you write, but be what you write about it.

Up next: let's brand your book

7

Brand Your Book

Okay! So! This section is going to talk about how to successfully brand your book on social media.

Now, this may sound redundant, but hear me out. While you have a brand as an *author*, you'll want to build a mini-brand for your *book*. Because there are so many other authors who share the same genre as you, you'll need to develop a plan of action to help your book capture the attention of your potential readers.

While you may know who resonates with you as an author, every book that you write won't always catch the interest of your audience. Because of that, you'll want to not only brand your platform, but also your book.

So, what exactly does it mean to build a mini-brand for your book? It means to create a movement that specifically corresponds with the message of the book that you'll be publishing. The simplest and most effective way to make this happen is through social media.

As we discussed in a previous chapter, your brand is how you'll be identified by your audience. And social media is one of the *easiest* ways to get exposure for books *and* to gain a new audience. But! You'll need a really great branding strategy for your book first.

Before we move forward, I need you to understand that having a brand is one of the *most* important parts about being an authorpreneur. Cool? Cool!

Brand Your Book on Social Media

Every aspiring and new author should not only utilize social media, but maximize it. Social media is the easiest way to promote your book and author platform. And my favorite part about this type of promotion is that it's free.99! It costs you $0.00 to set up a profile and to share information about you and your book. There are hundreds of authors who have sold quite a few books from social media posts, and you can, too.

Now, as with anything, there's a method to the digital madness. You have to be crafty about branding your book on social media. While all social media platforms have a common thread, each platform operates a little differently, so you'll need to know what you're working with so you can move accordingly.

We're going to discuss how to explicitly engage on Instagram and Facebook. These two platforms have been very successful for self-published authors. And once you implement these strategies, you'll see why.

Instagram. I really, *really* like Instagram for authors. Many authors haven't perfected this platform yet, so let's discuss how we can do that.

Instagram is a great platform for authors because it's all about images and visuals. What's more visual than a book cover?! You have the ability to gain quite a few new readers using this social media platform. The key is to create visually appealing graphics that represents the core message for your book and signature message for your brand.

I'm going to assume that you've already clearly identified both. If not, please, please, please do so before going forward.

When it comes to using and creating promotional graphics, be strategic and creative. Use images that will tell your brand's story without you having to be too wordy. Or use catchy quotes that captures the attention of your ideal readers.

Canva.com is a great tool to use to create free and eye-catching graphics. Fiverr.com also has some very affordable designers who will create book mock ups for under $10.

Once you get the visual part down, now you want to focus on your content. I recommend using pieces of your book's content as a status. Remember: re-purpose, re-purpose, re-purpose!

Lastly, your hashtag game! I can't tell you how many people I've connected with through a hashtag. Don't sleep on this part! Below are some hashtags that you can use when you promote your book on IG:

#author	#bookpromotion
#authorflow	#goodreads
#authorpreneur	#weekendreads
#aspiringauthor	#newbook
#newauthor	#fiction
#futureauthor	#nonfiction

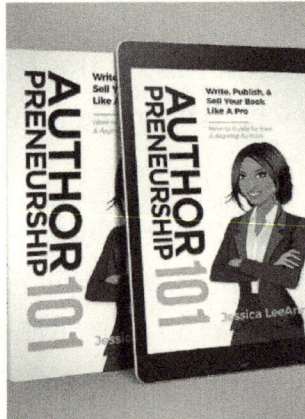

BUY MY BOOK NOW! AVAILABLE ON AMAZON!#BOOK #EBOOK #NEWBOOK #BOOKSFORWOMEN

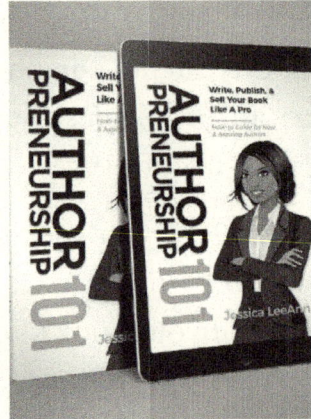

Have you had a chance to check out "Your book title here"? Learn 3 ways to "mention the benefits of your book". Now available on Amazon & Kindle. *Link in bio*

#book #ebook #booksforbrands #branding #Amazon #kindle #newbook

Now that you have some strategies on how to successfully post on Instagram, let's see how a great post should look. Below you'll see the right way and wrong way to post images on Instagram.

As you can see, the right way to post on Instagram is to use your caption box only for content. You'll put your hashtags in the comment section. This way your followers will focus on the content and not your hashtags. And please don't use caps. Create your posts to sound conversational, not salesy or pushy.

Facebook. One of my favorite things about Facebook is that there is no limit on the characters that you can post. However, try not to be too long winded. I know this can be hard, but try.

When posting on Facebook about your book, use one of the following formulas:

> ➤ Tell a story that ties into the message of your book.

> ➤ Share a review from a reader.

> ➤ Convey 3-5 nuggets readers will get from your book.

> ➤ And of course: post an image of your book!

Let's go over some examples of Facebook posts for authors. Keep in mind, your goal is to get readers to engage with your posts and turn them into customers.

Tell a story.

I remember feeling not so pretty because of my dark skin. It took me a long time to learn how to love myself. Now that I'm older, I have embraced my dark brown skin. I wrote Melanie the Melanin Queen to inspire black teen girls to embrace their unique beauty. Visit bit.ly/themelaninqueen to order your teen boo her copy today.

This example is why it's important to define your core message. I took the message from my young adult novel, *Melanie the Melanin Queen*, and shared why teens should read this book. Whenever I create these posts I see an increase of book sales.

Share a review.

"This is a dope and inspirational story. Very empowering for black teen girls. It should be on the nightstand of every black girl in America. Great read!" - Alika T.

Posting your book reviews is a great conversation starter on Facebook. This allows you to connect with potential readers who are interested in the topic of your book. This also gives you an opportunity to share your book link, which of course will bring attention to your book.

Provide 3-5 nuggets from your book.

After reading Melanie the Melanin Queen, teens will:

> *Understand what melanin is*

> *Have a better understanding of true friendship*

> *Will have a desire to chase their dream*

When potential readers have a better understanding of what your book is about, or why you think it will benefit them, they'll be more inclined to purchase a copy of your book.

Know this: nothing is off limits when it comes to marketing, promoting, and branding your book. Be as transparent, creative, and unique as your conscious will allow you to be.

Up next: let's position your brand

8

Position Your Brand

Your book is written. Your brand is developed. BOOM! Now it's time for the world to see your hard work! It's time to introduce your book and your brand to the world in a major way. It's time to position your brand.

So let's talk about what it looks like to position your author brand in front of the right readers. What's the point of doing this? Well, positioning your brand will bring the exposure to your core message, as well as your book, thus increasing your book sales and given your brand some attention.

Don't forget, in order to attract your ideal readers, you'll need to make your author brand visible. Your author brand is the foundation of your literary career. Brands sell books. *Not* book titles.

Sure, you want to have a great and catchy title, but if you want to turn your book into a business (which most authors desire to do) than you'll want to make sure your author brand is polished, professional, and also properly positioned.

So! How can an author position their author brand in front of the right readers? I'm so happy to tell you how! Next, we'll go over three proven ways every author should go about positioning their brand.

Now, these will not be new techniques or anything difficult to achieve. However, they are key and instrumental when it comes to your brand being visible and relevant. So let's talk about them.

Book Interviews

When you request interviews, make sure that you are working with organizations and outlets that represent the message of your brand. Before most interviews, the host will send you a list of questions that they'll ask. This gives you the opportunity to prepare your answers. You want to make sure that you're doing the interview to provide value. Don't focus on promoting your book, but rather sharing insight about your brand's core message. Here are four techniques that can help you provide value in your interviews:

➤ **Be confident**. You were booked because of the wisdom and insight that you have about the topic of your book, core message, or theme of the organization or outlet you're speaking with. You want to establish yourself as the go-to expert. People are drawn to confidence. Make sure that you answer questions with assurance.

➤ **Be timely**. If the interview starts at three o' clock, be on the call or at the location at 2:45. This will let the interviewer know that you're professional, you respect their time, and you're appreciative of the opportunity.

➤ **Be prepared**. Make sure you have water, tea or coffee if you'll need these things to get through your interview. Turn your cell phone off; be alert. Go over your questions and answers before the interview so you're not saying "um" or having to take too much time to think about your response.

➤ **Be entertaining**. Sure, you want to be serious about your craft and business. However, it's nothing wrong with having a little fun! Make appropriate jokes or laugh when the interviewer makes a joke. Be present, charming, and enjoy yourself.

Now that you have an idea of how to present yourself when being interviewed, get your media kit or one sheet ready and get booked! There are people waiting to hear how you can add some value to their lives.

Social Media

I'm a *huge* fan of marketing and promoting products and services on social media. It's free and it's unlimited possibilities. However, when it comes to positioning your brand on social media, you're going to need to be strategic. This means making sure the things you post are in alignment with your brand's core message. Sure, you can post pictures of your family and having a good time, but the bulk of your posts should be about your brand. Noticed I said *brand*, and not book. Use social media as a tool to connect with your ideal readers. When you're connected with them, they'll be more inclined to buy your books. Here are four strategies to help you successfully position your brand on social media:

> ➤ **Post 2x daily**. There's a rule of thumb when it comes to positing on social media as a business or brand. You don't have to flood your timeline with posts to get attention. Create a minimum of two posts daily that allows your

readers to engage with you. Don't exceed four posts a day about your book or brand.

➢ **Engage with your followers**. When you create a post, try to include a call to action or ask a question. Your goal is to get the people who you're connected with to engage in a conversation. This makes you more approachable and likeable, which can turn your followers into customers.

➢ **Schedule your posts**. If you're like most authors, you have a pretty busy life outside of accomplishing your literary goals. You may not have the time, or energy, to create social media posts as frequently as you'd like. If this is you, then I have some news for you: you can schedule your posts! There are a few apps that can help you out such as:
  o *Hootsuite*
  o *SproutSocial*
  o *Loomly*
  o *Zoho*

➢ **Invest in ads**. One of my favorite things about social media is that it's free. But I have to admit, I also like that there's an option to reach my ideal readers on a larger scale. How is this accomplished? By creating paid ads. Now, don't get intimated by this. You don't have to spend hundreds of dollars to connect with your ideal readers right away. You can create a $25 ad and get your post eyeballed by a specific group of people who are interested in your book and brand. Not sure how to make this happen? You know I got you! Here are four courses that will teach you how to create ads on social media for the low:

- o https://blog.reedsy.com/learning/cour ses/marketing/facebook-ads-authors/
- o http://www.viperchill.com/blueprint/
- o https://www.udemy.com/social-media-monitoring-for-business/
- o https://www.skillshare.com/classes/

Since we're talking about social media, let's quickly go over the best platforms for authors and why:

- *Facebook.* This platform is good for authors because it allows you to use content to connect.
- *Instagram.* This platform is good because it allows you to share images of your book cover, as well as images that reflect the message of your author brand.

- *LinkedIn.* This platform allows you to connect with professionals who may be interested in interviewing you about your brand, or connect with you for speaking engagements, etc.
- *Twitter.* This platform is good because it allows you to interact with other authors, and get your creative marketing juices flowing.

So now that you know how you can position your brand on social media, which one of these strategies will you implement within the next thirty days?

Word of Mouth

Okay so, networking aka word of mouth, is by far one of the most powerful ways to position your brand in the marketplace. This can be a tricky method, but it's effective. When you know exactly what to say, and how to say it, you'll leave people wanting to learn more about what you have to say. I know, talking about your book or author brand can seem a little vain. At any rate, if you don't speak passionately about what you're interested in, who else is going to vouch for you? The key is to surround yourself with people who are like-minded and are also striving to grow and establish their author brand or sell their book. When the topic of business and branding arises, make sure you provide invaluable advice that makes people want to hear more. Here are four ways to successfully get people interested in your book or author brand by word of mouth:

➢ **Be stimulating**. When you meet someone who shows a glimmer of interest in your book or brand, use your charisma and be thought-provoking. Leave them salivating and wanting more of what you have to say.

➢ **Be passionate**. Don't be afraid to exude your emotions about your book or brand. People love to see passion behind books, brands, and businesses. Many people have retained investors merely from their level of passion.

➢ **Be friendly**. Sure, you need to be professional, after all, being an author is about business. Nevertheless, show the people that you're talking to that you're human. Don't be robotic. Be fluid, fun, and friendly.

➢ **Be informative**. When you're out networking and rubbing elbows with like-minded people, this is the time to show off what you know. Don't just share your core message or passion, but include facts. Remember, in their eyes, you're an expert on the topic of your book or core message of your brand. Throw those facts out there and hook them with some valuable insight about what you know.

I know that it can be a little scary putting yourself out there. But if you never take that leap of faith, you'll never get the opportunity to talk about your book, let alone sell copies of your book. People will be drawn to your confidence, passion, and core message. Hone these traits and I promise that you'll begin to see the literary success you dream of.

Positioning your author brand is about connecting with your ideal audience, and getting potential readers excited about the message of your book. Branding is all about drawing people in. Keep them enticed, interested, and intrigued with your core message. Sure, they'll buy your book if they're interested. But don't you want people to buy your book to be impacted and transformed on a deeper level? If so, focus on building a brand that will enrich the lives of the people and community you're connected to. Make sure you create content that pierces hearts, and that you take the time to expose your brand to the people who will benefit from it the most.

9

Market Your Book

The biggest step that majority of all authors miss is not having a thorough and well-thought out marketing strategy for their book.

Before you publish your book, create an in-depth marketing plan. This will help reduce any anxiety you'll have about promoting and selling your book. Do your research and find out what methods other successful authors have used and tweak it to fit your brand or genre. I would recommend creating a marketing plan 60-90 days out so that you can focus on building your brand and growing your reader fan base.

Understanding the Marketing Process

When most authors hear the word marketing, they automatically associate this with promotion. While promotion is a huge part of marketing, it's not the foundation.

Marketing starts with understanding who your audience is so that you can develop a message that caters to their wants, needs, and desires. This includes the actual development of your book, how you will distribute the book, who you will sell it to, and how you will sell it to them.

Sounds like a lot, right?

Well, that's because it is. But! Don't let this frustrate or overwhelm you. It's important for you to understand what this means so that you can get it right. Answer these vital questions and you'll be able to create the perfect book marketing plan for your brand:

> *Will you focus on off line or online book sales first?*
> *How much money can you spend on promoting your book?*
> *What price will your target audience be willing to pay?*
> *Does your book cover convey the message of your content?*
> *How often will you promote your book?*
> *How will you connect with your readers?*

Answering these questions will make it a lot easier for you when you start the promotion part of your marketing plan. When you have a plan, you'll see results. So, let's talk about how you can market the book, now that you understand how and why.

Five Ways to Market Your Book

When most people decide that they're going to publish their book, the last thing that crosses their mind is how they're going to market their finished work to the world. Since this isn't at the forefront of a new author's mind, they often drop the ball on this part of the publishing process. I cannot stress the importance of having a solid, strategic marketing plan for your book. I mean, how else will the world know that you wrote a masterpiece?

So! Below you'll find the five most popular ways that you can market your books.

Local Book Signings. Don't despise small beginnings! A great, and fun way, to tell the masses about your book is through hosting book signings in your area. Putting together a book signing is not as difficult as you'd think. Reach out to the bookstores and libraries in your neighborhood and inquire about the process of hosting your own book signing. They'd be happy to help a new and local author.

Distribute Your Media Kit. So, what exactly is a media kit? It's a packet of information that includes all the details about your book and who you are as an author. It's primarily used to get the attention of the media, such as newspaper, television, and radio. Send your media kit to local newspapers, television and radio stations to bring exposure to your book.

Solicit Book Clubs. Book clubs are always looking for new books and authors for their monthly meet ups. Perform a google search to find book clubs that are interested in your book genre. Can't find one? Then start your own! Get a group of readers together to discuss your book and share reviews on social media.

Use Social Media. Social media is one of the most powerful, free marketing tools any author can utilize. You can reach thousands, millions of people who are interested in what you write about. Be sure to be consistent. Don't be scared to use paid ads to find your target readers. I highly recommend doing so.

Tell Everyone You Know! Yes! Brag about your book! Okay, maybe not brag, but don't be shy about telling people that you wrote an amazing book. Word of mouth is the best way to reach a new audience.

You'd be surprised at how many people would purchase a copy or two of your book if you tell them all about. So start talking!

Now that you have five solid ways to market your book, let's discuss how we can get your book noticed on a local, regional, *and* national level. This is going to take some strategic planning in the form of gaining publicity. There are four areas that you want to cover when you're taking the ever so complex publicity route. Let's chop it up about that now.

Four Points of Publicity

There are many different components that an author needs to understand in order to achieve literary success. One of them is publicity. Publicity is usually associated with celebrities, but it's a tool for entrepreneurs, and authorpreneurs, as well. So publicity - what exactly does that word mean? Well, it's a mixture of four key elements that you'll need to implement as you're building your career as an author. Its main definition is being noticed by someone in the media or local press. However, before you can get noticed or recognition from the media or press, you'll need to have the following elements in place.

Branding. As an author, when building a brand, you have to develop a strong sense of who you are as a writer and display it to your readers. Whether it's online or offline, when people hear your name, key words should come to mind. Branding is about putting your stamp on everything that you do, write, or talk about. It's how your readers will connect with you.

Marketing. I know that most authors confuse marketing with promotion, but today I want you to stop being one of those authors! Marketing isn't about telling people to buy your book, it's about the *way* that you tell them to buy your book. It's having a targeted audience in place and strategically informing them about your book in a way that persuades them to buy it.

Promotion. Now, promotion is about sharing your book with your target audience. It's how you will inform your readers where and how to buy your book. So, before you encourage people to buy your book, you first have to define your target market. Once you have a great marketing strategy in place, then you promote to your market. Make sense?

Publicity. Now that you've branded yourself, developed your marketing strategy, and are promoting to your target audience, it's time to level up! You can now position your platform in front of the right people by garnering publicity for your brand. You noticed I didn't say book, but *brand*. Why? Because people will buy your book simply because they're vested in your brand. If you have an impactful brand, you'll sell books.

Okay, can we have a truth moment? When you decided to write a book you had no clue that it was a business, huh? Yeah, me either! I learned everything that I needed to know later in my journey. However, once I learned what I needed to get the success I was chasing, some amazing things begin to happen. And I want to teach you how to do the same, without having to take the long route that I took.

I want you to know that this journey will not be easy, but it's a lot of fun and worth it. Don't just focus on selling books, but actually impacting the readers who indulge in your book. Whether you write fiction or nonfiction, your voice matters. If you're going to jump into the literary game, do it the right way, and for the right reasons.

10

Promote Your Book

Whether it's your first or tenth book, you'll need to have a great promotional plan. Your plan should include creating (or paying for) promotional tools. Your promotional tools should reflect that you're a professional, polished, and poised author. Image is everything. And you want to make sure you come out of the gate swinging with visual tools that establishes you as an author to reckon with.

Book promotion is all about positioning your book in front of the right people. In this chapter, we'll discuss the ways that you can bring exposure to your book though promotion.

Monetize Your Message

So! Let's talk book promotion strategies. Before I published my first book I had no clue how to go about being a successful author. All I knew is that being a best-selling author was a huge accomplishment and I wanted in! Now that I've been in the publishing industry for over ten years, I've learned that the process of becoming a best-selling author has changed and doesn't necessarily hold the same weight it did years ago. Sure, it's still a great accomplishment, but not as hard to achieve if you have the right tools and content.

You see, with self-publishing being the wave now, it's a lot easier to become a best-seller, well, at least according to Amazon sales. I also know that just because someone has that title under their belt doesn't mean that they're generating money. I know quite a few Amazon best-selling authors that still work a 9-5.

So how do authors actually make money? By monetizing their signature message. And what does that process look like? Glad you wanna know! Below are three ways that authors make money from their books.

Speaking engagements. Your book should be more than just a story. It should be a solution to someone's problem, even if it's fiction. Find three nuggets from your content and develop them into speaking topics so that you can book paid speaking engagements. Now, you may have to start off speaking for free, but that's okay. Use those opportunities to sharpen your speaking skills. Also, this will help you get new eyes on your book, and new book sales as well.

Group coaching programs. Most coaching programs were developed from someone's personal experiences. They wrote down all of the issues they experienced, and now teach others the strategies that they used to overcome that issue. You already have the content, re-purpose it and turn it into a program. Not only will you get to increase your sales, but you'll also get a chance to transform lives. There are many types of coaching programs you can create. Be open to this possibility.

Workshops and conferences. If you've already written a book or have the solution to a major problem that your target audience is facing, create a signature workshop or conference that provides the solution in an intimate setting. This will also give you the opportunity to promote your book in depth. I personally *love* workshops and conferences. It gives you an opportunity to connect with your tribe on a deeper level. It also helps you establish your brand in a specific community.

Being an authorpreneur is about taking your book and turning it into a business. The more avenues that you have to talk about your book, the more books you'll actually sell. Use your book as a path that leads you to other opportunities that will allow you to generate money from the message you write about.

Now that you know how to promote your book and monetize your message, let's chat about the tools you'll need to get some attention for that book of yours.

Marketing & Promotional Tools

When it comes to positioning your book in front of the right people, you'll need to grab their attention with marketing materials such as a press release, media kit, flyers, one sheet, post cards, bookmarks, and business cards - just to name a few. We mentioned these items earlier, but let's talk about what each of these documents mean, when you'll use them, and examples of what some of these tools should look like.

Press Release. A press release is a document that announces your book release or a local event. This is what you'll provide to local, regional, and national outlets that make announcements on behalf of authors. You can also use a press release to announce your book signing event.

A press release can be re-created each time that you have a new event, or want to get exposure for your book. You want to make sure that you include your book cover, contact information, a catchy title, a professional photo, and a great story that ties into the message of your book. Also include a review. Your press release should read like an in-depth book summary. It needs to be written in third person, and make it good!

See a press release on the following page

TEACHING BLACK TEENS HOW TO CONFIDENTLY EMBRACE THEIR BROWN SKIN

Press Release

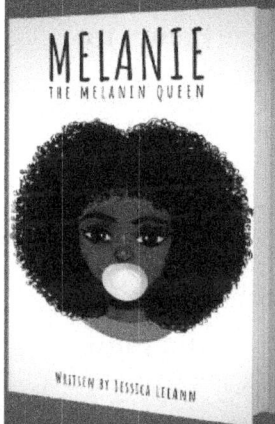

All through middle school Melanie Roberts was teased and bullied because of her melanated skin. It wasn't until she discovered the term "melanin" that she begin to understand and embrace her dark brown skin, as well as to see her own unique beauty.

Jessica LeeAnn vividly shares the journey of the 14 year old finding her self-confidence, falling in love for the first time, and embracing her brown skin. Readers will re-define their definition of beauty, feel inspired and empowered to be their authentic selves in a world that tries to teach them otherwise.

Melanie the Melanin Queen is an inspiring, thought-provoking, electrifying, and fun read.

Our young black girls need to understand and be aware of how beautiful they are, just being in the skin they're in. This book will reassure, redirect, and become a resource to the girl who has questions and has been doubtful as the result of being ridiculed and bullied because of the color of her skin.

-Widny Lherisson, inspirational blogger

Melanie the Melanin Queen
By Jessica LeeAnn
Paperback: 176 pages $9.99
ISBN: 13: 978-1719241069

Contact
Jessica LeeAnn
www.jessicaleeann.com

Jessica LeeAnn is a Bay Area native. She has authored 8 books, 3 of which are young adult books. She is passionate about empowering black teen girls to embrace their unique identity. Visit www.jessicaleeann.com to learn more.

Media Kit. A media kit is a set of promotional materials that provide information about an author which is distributed to the media and booksellers for publicity. You can use a graphic designing website such as Canva.com to help you create your own media kit. Or you can hire a freelance designer for a very affordable rate on a website such as Fiverr.com to create a unique and branded media kit. See below for a checklist of items that are included in a media kit.*

- ➤ **Author Bio.** Write an overview of your life and writing career in the third person.
- ➤ **Book Synopsis.** Write an in-depth summary of your book. Make sure you write in the third person as well.
- ➤ **Press Release.** See previous section.
- ➤ **Book Excerpt.** Choose a portion of one of the chapters in your book.
- ➤ **Interview Questions.** Choose ten questions that will be conversation starters for interviews that you book.
- ➤ **Contact Information.** Include your email address, website, social media handles, and if you're comfortable, your phone number.
- ➤ **Shell Sheet.** Include of the details about your book: page count, size, genre, price, ISBN, publisher, etc.
- ➤ **Photos.** Include professional, high-resolution head shots. You will also need a photo of your

book cover. I recommend using a 3d book cover.

See below for example of a Media Kit.

Press Release   04

Did you spend all of 2018 watching your friends buy the thing you want or take the vacations you...

Your 2019 year
how to respons
Financial Coach
of experience in
Your Money. Fe
hard way about
get her finances
of as a young gir

R.O.C.K Your M
leisure of learni
will teach wome
effectively chan
finances.

This powerful b
intended to get
to create a bette
Potential, Own
Story, and Know
striving to thriv

Bio   03

Felicia V. Petit-Frere (Coach Fe) is the CEO of Windsong Financial Coaching LLC. With 22 years of corporate financial experience and a lifetime of personal financial experience, Felicia is the expert to seek when in financial turmoil. She has been helping friends and family become financially fit for a couple of years before she officially started her business. Her #1 goal for her business is to teach women how to responsibly manage their finances. She believes that everyone makes unfortunate financial deci...

Contents

Contact Felicia   07

Book Excerpt   06

Understanding Your Credit Report

Okay, let's have a truth moment: if you want to borrow money from any sort of financial establishment (except a payday loan company), your credit report must be reviewed. Your credit report gives the lender a snapshot of your financial history and may be accessed by potential employers, lenders and department stores. The information in your credit report det...

Sell Sheet   05

MEDIA KIT FOR
Felicia V. Petit-Frere

Title: R.O.C.K. Your Money
Author: Felicia V. Petit-Frere
Genre: Self-help
Price: $14.99
# of Pages: 144
ISBN: 9781793015051
Available on Amazon & Kindle

One Sheet. This is a one page sell sheet that talks about who you are, your book summary, and includes your signature message. It also includes your contact information.

A One Sheet, also known as a Speaker One Sheet, is used to give an organization or company a snapshot of the value you'll bring to their platform. It's a very condensed version of your Media Kit. You'll need similar elements, but not all.

This type of document will be good to book interviews or speaking engagements prior to a book release. It doesn't have to be as dramatic as a Media Kit, it just needs to highlight the most important aspects of your book and brand message.

See an example on the following page.

> I teach my clients how to write powerful books and build authentic author brands from scratch.

Jessica LeeAnn

Author | Entrepreneur | Literary Coach

Jessica LeeAnn is an established author, publishing consultant, and a literary coach. She is the CEO of Chocolate Readings, which is a literary and author development firm for women & men of color. Jessica teaches new and aspiring authors how to successfully write, publish, and sell their book to their ideal readers, as well as how to build their brand from scratch.

Keynote Topics

- Branding Your Author Platform
- Power of Social Media
- Launch Your Book Like a Pro

Connect with Jessica LeeAnn

Website: www.chocolatereadings.com
Email: jessica@chocolatereadings.com

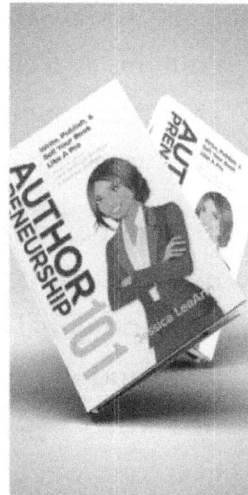

There are so many additional branding tools that you can use to help your brand stand out. Success leaves clues, so I recommend that you check out other successful authors and see what branding tools their using and what's working for them. Be creative, original, use color, and make sure your tools align with the message of your book.

Now, let's chop it up about another way to promote your book: blogging!

Are You Blogging?

Okay! Blogs are the *easiest* way for authors to promote their content. I briefly mentioned blogging in Chapter 1 as a way for aspiring authors to conquer their content, as well as connect with your target audience. I want to touch on why you should have a blog, and four ways you can get your blog poppin'.

I personally believe that every author, aspiring, new or seasoned, should have a blog. Your blog will show potential readers two things: 1) the content you write and 2) your writing style. No matter how dope of a writer you are, your book isn't for everyone. Not everyone will connect with your style of writing, and that's okay. Having a blog will allow potential readers to determine if it's worth the investment to buy your book. It's also a great way to build your mailing list.

The main reason every author should have a blog is because it's a great way to build readership. If someone enjoys your blog posts, they're more likely to buy your books when you launch them. You may think, *"What in the world can I say on a blog post?"* A LOT!

Here are four ways that you can keep your blog interesting:

1. If your book is already published, share a short excerpt. Talk about why the excerpt you chose is relevant in that moment.
2. If your book is not published, share why you're writing a book and how it will be useful for your potential readers.
3. Share your experience writing your first book. This is a great way to connect with your target audience.
4. Share your favorite quote and three ways it's helped you grow or evolve. Doing this will show your readers that you're relatable.

There are plenty of other topics you can talk about on your blog. Share you experiences and expertise. People love learning new things, and feeling connected to people who share similar interests. Remember, as an author, you want to position yourself as the expert in your field or genre. Having a blog will do this. You can also interview other people that share the same genre/core message as you. A blog will also help you expand your network.

Up next: let's get your book noticed

11

Get Your Book Noticed

Okay! So on to the good stuff! The book is published, you know who it's for, and you've been building your brand, now it's time to get your book into the hands of your ideal readers. There are several ways to get your book noticed and we'll talk about that in the next few pages.

Know this: you'll need a marketing plan, marketing tools, a team of dedicated people, and an insane work ethic to get it done.

First up: let's talk about having (or becoming) a publicist.

Do I Really Need a Publicist?

In the previous chapter, we talked a little bit about publicity. Now let's dig deeper and talk about what exactly it means to get and have a publicist.

Most authors think that if they have a publisher, that this will help them get the exposure they're looking for. This isn't necessarily the case. A publisher is solely responsible for distributing your book to bookstores and online booksellers. Depending on the type of company you're signed with or hire, some companies will provide you with promotional materials, advertisements, and get book reviews. But that's about it. They're not responsible for marketing your book. You are.

I'm going to repeat that last statement because this isn't truly understood: your publisher is *not* responsible for marketing your book. You are.

When it comes down to positioning your book in front of your ideal readers, you'll want to hire help. This is where a publicist comes into play. So, what exactly is a publicist? Someone who will coordinate (or help you coordinate) your book signings, marketing campaigns, help you get interviews, etc.

A publicist will be responsible for pitching your book and author brand to magazines, radio, TV, bloggers, and podcast hosts. Your publicist will help you develop a marketing plan that makes sense for your book and author brand. They'll also help you create your press release and media kit, and help you turn your book into a brand by strategically marketing your message.

Why do you need a publicist? To help your ideal readers find your book. As a first time author, I encourage you to hire one, or learn how to do this skill yourself. Publicists can be pricey, but worth it if you want to turn your book into a business.

Now, keep in mind that working with a publicist will not bring you overnight success. It will, however, prepare you for the journey of establishing your author brand in front of the right people and get your book exposed to the marketplace.

Three Ways to Get Your Book Noticed

Okay, let's be real for a second here. Maybe hiring a publicist isn't in your budget just yet, and I get it. Don't stress, I'll share three ways that you can position your book in front of your readers without a publicist. But! When you get the coins to hire a publicist, do it!

So, what other ways can you get your book noticed? By re-purposing your content. Let's talk about what that means, and three ways you can do this.

Re-purposing your book's content is when you share your message in different formats to different platforms. One of the most important aspects of being an authorpreneur is mastering this activity.

One of my favorite things about re-purposing content is that it can be done in many different forms. Thanks to technology, we now have multiple ways of getting out content into the marketplace, on and off line.

The best way to determine which path is best for you and your brand is to find out where you ideal reader spends their time. Some key ways to learn this is by asking questions: *How do they like to receive re-purposed content? Which method resonates with them more?*

Once you understand what your readers want, you can create content specific to their need and deliver it to them in the vehicle that they're most attracted to.

I've found that there are three main ways to share re-purposed content that can grab the attention of your tribe. You can either *write* content, *share* content on social media, or *host* a live event using your signature content.

Depending on the nature of your brand, focus on selecting one format that works best for you and *work* it! Feel free to incorporate other forms; however, it's always best to stick with what works for your platform.

Okay, so let's get to it!

Written Content. There are so many ways to share written content and I love it! This is by far one of the most stable and consistent ways of getting your content in front of the right people. It's also the most prolific. How many people have you connected to from reading something that grabbed your attention? Lots, right?! Here are the most popular ways to share written, re-purposed content:

➢ *Blog posts*
➢ *Email marketing campaigns*
➢ *Newsletters*
➢ *Magazine articles*
➢ *Workbooks*

Digital Content. While people love to read, they also love to watch and/or listen to content as well. This format is best for the chatty Cathy's of the world (*like me, hehe*). Live streaming is one of the most popular and quickest ways to provide your tribe with your re-purposed content. All you have to do is clear your throat, press record, smile, and let the content flow from your lips. Here are the most popular platforms for sharing digital content:

➢ *Periscope*
➢ *Facebook Live*
➢ *Snapchat*
➢ *Instagram Live*
➢ *YouTube*
➢ *Webinars*
➢ *Audio books*

Live Events. What do all people have in common? *Connecting!* We *love* to gather, laugh, talk and share information with each other. Facilitating a live event is one of the most fun ways of re-purposing your content – through speaking. While this may be the most costly way of getting content to your tribe, it's also one of, if not the most, interactive and effective ways of connecting with like-minded individuals. Here are the most popular types of events you can host:

➢ *Workshops*
➢ *Mastermind groups*
➢ *Intensives*
➢ *Boot camps*
➢ *Retreats*
➢ *Conferences*
➢ *Seminars*
➢ *Symposiums*

Re-purposing content doesn't have to be boring or dull. It doesn't have to be long and drawn out, either. There are plenty of ways to share your expertise as well as many ways to find your target audience in a way that brings life to your passion. With a little research, proofreading, good editing, and impactful lessons to share, your content should successfully fulfill its purpose.

12

Launch Your Book

Now, here is the fun part about being an author: the book launch! Yes, it's time to introduce your book to the world. Whoop, whoop!

The book launch process is where *all* of the hard work, money, and fear that you've experienced over the last few months (some of you years) will finally pay off.

Launching your book has a few different parts, which includes the publishing process and having a book signing.

The one thing you have to, *have to* do is have a book signing. You just *have* to! It's so much fun to talk about your new book with readers. Also, it will really bring the experience as an author full circle.

In this chapter, we'll go over the tools and resources you'll need to successfully launch your book like a pro! Ready?

You Need a Website & Mailing List

As you know by now, I am a *huge* advocate for authors branding themselves and positioning their platform in front of the right readers. One of the ways that you can do this is by having a website.

A website is your digital business card. It's your own portal that allows you to share your content freely. Don't get me wrong, I love social media, but those platforms have restrictions. Having a website allows you to build a unique and creative platform to engage with your readers. You want to have a website so that you can have a space where your target audience can connect with you off of social media and after live events. Your website helps you to have brand consistency.

Now that you know why you should have a website, let's talk about how you'll utilize it.

The main thing you'll utilize your website for is to sell your book. You don't want to rely on Amazon and book stores to be the only resource people can get your book. Selling your own book will also allow you to keep more of your royalties. The other reason is to continue the literary convo you started in your book. You'll do this with blogs, videos, and my personal favorite- an email list.

What's an email list? It's another form of marketing. What you want to do is capture the email addresses of people who are interested in your book or who have already bought your book. You want to have a mailing list so that you can nurture the relationship with potential and existing readers. Plus, these will be the first people that you get to market your new books, products, and services to.

So, how does having a website and mailing list help with a book launch? It's a marketing tool! Before you launch your book, you'll want to market and promote it to potential readers. You'll use your website to talk about your book and capture email addresses so that when your book is available, you'll already have a list of people who will turn into customers.

When it comes to developing your website, you can do one of two things: hire someone or create one yourself. While I strongly urge you to hire a professional, if you are tech-savvy, you can also create your own. Companies like Wix, Wordpress, and Shopify have ready-made templates that makes it easy for individuals to create their own website. You can get a pretty reasonably priced website created for about $300. If you can't afford a full website, you can get what is called a Landing Page or a 1-Page website for about $100.

Now, as for the email list I mentioned. There are a few different options you can work with. If you have a Wix, Wordpress, or Shopify website, you can build your mailing list within the platform. You can also utilize email marketing software such as MailChimp, AWeber or Ontraport. I like MailChimp for new authors because it's free for up to 2,000 email subscribers. Of course, I encourage you to do your research and choose the best option for your brand and budget.

Whichever software you choose to use, just make sure that you are consistent with connecting with your mailing list. You can either email them on a weekly or monthly basis. Please don't flood their inbox daily about your book. They'll get annoyed and will unsubscribe.

As a first-time author, you can start with a monthly newsletter. Once you get comfortable and confident, level up and send an email weekly. Remember, keep your readers engaged so they'll keep your brand at the forefront of their busy minds.

Building Your Book Launch Team

So! The big day is approaching and it's time to get your team together to help you promote your new book. Exciting right? Right!

There is a strategic way to make this happen and we're going to cover that in this next section. You have the website, you have some emails, now let's build the team who will help you get your book the attention it deserves. So, let's dig in!

What is a Launch Team? A launch team is a group that you will recruit to help bring exposure to your book. This will be your book promotion team. The people you recruit must be passionate about the message of your book or genuinely want to see you succeed as an author. As the saying goes: Team work, makes the dream work!

Why You Need a Launch Team? Your launch team is responsible for helping you get reviews, and to share your book. Your team is responsible for reading the book before it launches and post a review during the first week your book is published. The more reviews, the better chance you have at ranking high in book categories on Amazon and other online retailers.

How to Create a Launch Team? Reach out to 15-30 people that you know are reliable. You want to choose people who can commit to reading your book and provide a review during the week of your launch. You will communicate with your team about when, what, and how to implement your plan of action.

When to Start your Book Launch? You want to recruit your launch team 30-45 days before your release date. You want to give your team time to read your book so they can provide a review. Keep in mind, your team doesn't have to read your entire your book. If you want, you can give them a few chapters. Just be sure to give them enough content to provide a solid review.

Guidelines for Your Launch Team. Now that you know why you need a launch team and when to start the process, you want to create some guidelines; you want to have a plan of action for them to follow. One thing I learned is that people work better when they have all of the ins and outs of a specific process. When people know what to expect, that's less time you'll have to spend explaining what needs to be done, and you can focus your energy on having a successful launch.

Incentives for your Launch Team. As a thank you to your team, be sure to provide them with some incentives to encourage them to fully participate in your launch. You can provide services and products that are in alignment with your book as an incentive, or you can purchase a small gift to show your token of appreciation.

Build Your Launch Team Master Checklist. Okay! Now that you know what it takes to get your launch team together, create a checklist of what you'll need to successfully launch your book so you're not running around like a chicken with its head cut off. Remember, you need to stay focused during your launch.

Whew! That was a *lot*, right? Well, now you know exactly what it takes to position your book in front of the right readers. It's not easy, but it's possible when you have a plan.

I remember having a conversation with one of my clients and after I explained this process to her she replied, "This is a lot of work! I just wanted to be an author." This is what it takes to be an author. The reason why it looks so easy, is because most authors have a team of people helping them, i.e. a book launch team.

Host a Book Signing

Okay, now on to the next phase of launching your book: the book signing.

I would be remiss to not talk about the importance of having a book signing. *Hello*! This is by far the *best* part of being an author! To share your passion project with the world.

So! Once you officially and successfully launch your book, you'll want to host a live event by way of a book signing. It baffles me when I speak with aspiring authors and they ask if they should have a book signing. Um, *yes*! Yes, you should.

Hosting your own book signing is a huge part of marketing and promoting your book. If you don't stand in front of crowds of people with your book in hand, many people won't know that you exist.

Now, a lot of new authors look past this step because we're in the digital era and most people are crushing online sales. And that's amazing! However, don't overlook the local, regional, and national sales. This entails you going out into communities and hosting book signings. This also gives you the opportunity to make connections with book store owners, libraries, and organizations that support the message of your book.

I know that having a book signing can seem a little intimidating, but it's a fairly simple process. Here's a quick checklist of the things you'll need to host a successful book signing:

1. **Choose a venue**. Don't get so caught up in having a book signing at a book store. Other options are the library, a hotel or community center meeting rooms, small coffee shops, or restaurants. Also, take into consideration what type of book you're writing. For example: if it's a religious book, maybe you can ask your church.

2. **Choose a date and time**. You want to make sure that you choose a date and time that most people can attend. Most people don't mind going to a book signing in the evenings. However, choosing a weekend date could be more profitable for you. Also, your signing shouldn't go over two hours.

3. **Have a plan**. Create a format that you feel most comfortable talking about your book. My favorite format to host a book signing is to read an excerpt and ask the crowd 3-4 questions about the excerpt I've read out loud. Another format I like is to have a panel and ask them

questions surrounding the message of the book to give the attendees a better understanding of how to apply the content in the book to their own journeys.

4. **Order your books and materials**. Give yourself time for your books and promotional materials to arrive. 2-4 weeks is plenty of time for you to make sure your books and materials such as banners, book marks, post cards, and flyers are on hand and available on the day of your event.

5. **Have different payment methods**. With PayPal, Square, Stripe, Venmo, and CashApp being payment methods that are acceptable, make sure that you not only have these apps, but also cash so you can refund customers who may purchase your books with large bills.

6. **Have fun!** Be creative and do an activity or exercise that will get your attendees to engage with you. You can have a contest, play a game, or do a raffle. You want people to not only buy your book, but enjoy themselves as well.

So, now that you have a quick checklist of how to facilitate a book signing, I want you to make sure you take action and follow through. Don't be overwhelmed or anxious with the process. Just focus on being prepared and have fun!

As stated at the beginning of this chapter, launching your book has a few components, and all of these components need to be fulfilled in order to have a successful launch. Now, a successful launch doesn't mean becoming a best-seller overnight. It means that you set the goal and reached said goal. The accolades are additional.

Now that you know all that it takes to have a successful book launch, are you ready to launch your new book like a pro?

I hope you know that you are. You have everything that it takes to be successful. You got this!

Final Thoughts....

As we're wrapping up *Authorpreneurship 101*, I'm going to share the most important tip for achieving literary success. Two simple words that will require simple action: be consistent.

This is how your favorite authors have reached their pinnacle of success. They remained consistent. They had a plan, stuck to it, and didn't give up. That is how you're reading this book. Because I made a choice to be consistent.

The reason why most aspiring and new authors drop the ball here is because of fear. Yep, the fear of the unknown. If you're going to become an authorpreneur, you're going to have to embrace fear. What do I mean by this? I mean that you're going to have to stop letting fear be a reason you don't move forward with writing, publishing, and selling your book.

And in the words of the amazing Lisa Nichols, "With knees knocking and teeth chattering, do it anyway!" I love when she says this! And it's true.

I was so nervous about writing this book. I thought, *What if I miss something? What if no one likes it?* I had to get over the fear of the outcome and just do it! And I'm so very glad that I did.

I know that this guide will help aspiring and new authors just like you take the first step towards accomplishing their literary goals. And I wish you *much* success as you do.

I have a lot of consultations with aspiring authors and one of the questions they often ask about is the process of becoming a best-seller or about other successful authors I've worked with. And here's the deal:

1. Not everyone defines success the same way. One author may view being successful as selling 1,000 copies of their book on a monthly bases vs. another author viewing success as simply accomplishing their publishing goal and using their book to get speaking engagements.

2. Not everyone is a best-seller because they wrote/published a good book. There is an unethical way that a lot of authors have made the Amazon best-sellers list. Also, becoming a true best-seller doesn't happen overnight. It takes time and a really great marketing strategy.

3. Your goal as a new author should include being a trailblazer. Sure, success leaves clues, but you can also be successful by blazing your own path. Don't put unnecessary pressure on yourself to get accolades. Focus on writing a really dope or impactful book.

Aspiring authors: please keep in mind that your literary journey will not be the same as others. You have to keep in mind that a lot of high-selling books are due to the genre and/or brand of the author. You can't compare yourself to a best-selling children's book and you're writing about being a broken divorcee. Those are two different readers, with two different strategies to get sales.

While I know that you have a story and you're extremely passionate about it, if your goal is to become a best-seller I recommend checking out what readers are interested in before you publish your book. And after you build a loyal fan of readers, then publish your passion book.

If you're not concerned with labels and online recognition (as you shouldn't be), focus on building your author brand, write your amazing, impactful book, and launch it like a pro!

Acknowledgements

I saw my granddaddy reading and taking notes on yellow legal pads for years when I was growing up. I never had the courage to ask him what he wrote about. Now that he's having conversations with God face to face, I can't ask, and won't ever know.

While I can't ask him, I feel that I'm carrying on his habit. My granddaddy was a dreamer. And so am I. Now as an author, editor, self-publishing consultant, and literary coach, I imagine that I'm living the dream my granddaddy wrote about on those legal yellow pads. I can't tell you how many journals and small notebooks that I have in my home, car, and purse. From time to time I think about my granddaddy, and smile. I imagine seeing his dimpled face smiling with me. Granddaddy, thank you for being a dreamer.

My granny was a librarian's assistant for most of my childhood. I remember that she'd bring home boxes of books from the Richmond Public Library, and my cousins and I would dig through the boxes and find books like *The Babysitters Club*, *Flyy Girl*, and *The Coldest Winter Ever* and read in our spare time. Without my granny's love of books, and desire for us to read, I don't know if I've ever would have taken up an interest in reading. Granny, you've inspired my journey in ways you'll never know. I love you sassy lady.

My mom is by *far* my biggest supporter. She's come to every literary event I've had (until I moved to Dallas, TX). Her support is the reason why I can't stop. I can't let her down. Thank you for being super woman.

My daughter has been so understanding watching me follow my dreams, and I appreciate her for not feeling neglected during the many late nights I've stayed up writing or coaching; and the Saturday afternoons I spend at events trying to make things happen. Chicky D, thank you for being *so* amazing.

I appreciate every coach, mentor, and leader I've been blessed to connect with over the years. Your words and actions have been the seeds of success that planted my drive, ambition, and determination to win. Thank you all for being obedient to the Divine call on your life and pushing me to do the same.

I also want to acknowledge the clients I've had thus far. You each have inspired me to grow and stretch myself beyond my mental capacity. Because of each of you, I dream harder, learn deeper, and teach from a place of love.

Lastly, I acknowledge and give all honor to the Most High for giving me one of the greatest gifts on earth: to selflessly share my gift. I had no clue that I'd be an author, editor, self-publishing consultant, literary coach, or any of the other things you've allowed me to be. I can't believe this is my *life*! I can't believe I get to do something that I'm passionate about each and every day. Who would have ever thought that a girl from Richmond, CA would write books, own a literary company, and teach countless of aspiring and new authors how to do something that she learned by trial and error. Yahweh, I will forever acknowledge you as my God and carry myself as your daughter. I love you for loving me enough to allow me to live out my dreams. I can't wait to see you again.

About the Author

Jessica LeeAnn is an author, editor, literary coach, and self-publishing consultant. She is also the founder and CEO of Chocolate Readings. Chocolate Readings is a literary and author development firm for men and women of color.

Jessica grew up in Richmond, California and currently resides in Dallas, Texas. She enjoys teaching aspiring authors how to successfully write, sell, and publish their books, as well as teach new authors how to turn their book into a profitable business.

Jessica developed workshops, courses, and trainings such as Writer's Flow, Self-Publishing for Beginners, Book Launch Bootcamp, and Marketing for Self-Published Authors to help authors learn how to successfully navigate in the literary industry. She also has an Author Accountability Group on Facebook, where she shares literary tips, tools, and techniques with her community. Her goal is to teach as many aspiring authors as she possibly can how to successfully write, publish, and sell their books like pros.

To leave a book review or to connect with Jessica LeeAnn, visit www.chocolatereadings.com

References

1. https://www.isbn-international.org/content/what-isbn

2. https://barcode-labels.com/solutions/upc-labels/book-labels/

3. https://publicityhound.com/blog/author-media-kit-include-8-essential-items

4. https://www.legalzoom.com/articles/how-to-copyright-a-book

5. https://www.amarketingexpert.com/rock-solid-book-marketing-2018/

6. https://mirandamarquit.com/how-should-you-charge-for-freelance-editing/

10560224R00090